Body Talk - Basic Mime

Body Talk - Basic Mime

By Mario Diamond

Copyright © 2019 by Modern Vaudeville Press

All rights reserved. This book or any portion thereof may not be reproduced or used in any manner whatsoever without the express written permission of the publisher except for the use of brief quotations in a book review.

Photographs by René Beaumier - cpgp3.com

ISBN 978-1-7339712-1-8

www.modernvaudevillepress.com

To Claude St-Denis, my silent mentor…

To anyone with a need to express themselves and cannot find the words.

To teach is to learn twice

Joseph Joubert

Contents

Foreword	vii
Introduction	ix
Definitions	1
Origins	3
Face	5
Hands	12
Body lines or Axes	17
Postures	27
Energy and movement	29
Visual effects	35
Pantomime	40
Improvisation	55
Other Titles by Modern Vaudeville Press	58

Foreword

The Art of Mime

The art of mime is the identification with the essence of all things, and the portrayal of thought and emotion through silent physical expression. A mime works with the laws of physics: weight, gravity, principles of motion and resistance and inertia. We move through space as a visible, tangible substance.

Mime training is different from other movement disciplines like dance and gymnastics. It is specific to the art of silent communication. Mario Diamond does a welcome service with this book, helping to promote the techniques and principles of our misunderstood and fragile art.

Rob Mermin

Rob Mermin studied mime with Marcel Marceau and Etienne Decroux, before embarking on a career as a mime and silent clown in theaters and circuses. To learn more about him and his work, visit www.RobMermin.com

Introduction

As a kid, I could not stop talking, with words as much as gestures. When my mother could not take it anymore, she would make me sit on my hands. It was magical, not one more sound would come out of my mouth. Later in life, I discovered talking was unnecessary. I could remain silent and still say so many things.

After trying dance, a beautiful discipline in which I was not that good, I tried theatre where I felt limited by the language. I needed to be able to communicate with the entire world. In 1976, I discovered mime through Vincent Marcotte, an incredible teacher. After only a few hours in class, I decided to become full time silent actor.

One year later, the master mime Claude St-Denis was playing in a theater close to where I lived. I needed to see how one person on stage, with no decor, no music and no props, could be interesting enough to keep an audience for an hour or longer. After the show, I was lucky to meet him and talk about silence. A few months later, I became his student and stage partner.

I am still performing on stage and using mime in different spheres. For example, playing physical characters in movies. Teaching has taken more and more space in my life. Using what I learned from elders and understanding that different students learn differently and that some need to learn more quickly, (especially when teaching techniques to those who will not become mimes,) I developed a teaching method and adapted mime techniques for circus artists, figure skaters, jugglers, magicians and even politicians.

Theory is important to feed your knowledge and practice makes you understand how to use it. In this book, I will explain the theory. It is up to you to explore and play.

Definitions

Mime

Acting without the use of speech. Using only your hands, facial expressions and body to communicate emotions and actions.

Mime

Mime is an art. A way to express yourself, just like dance, music, painting and other art forms. On stage, you are far from the audience. Your body becomes the microphone of everything you express.

Mime

The person who practices mime.

Origins

Mime is considered one of the earliest mediums of self-expression. Before there was spoken language, we can imagine mime was used to communicate.

Thousands of moons later, communicating through silence was developed in ancient Greece. History or legend says that the practice of mime, as we see it today, began at the Theater of Dionysus.

Centuries later, in 1816, a Bohemian acrobatic family was playing in Paris. The son of the family, Jean Gaspard Batiste Deburau, was engaged to perform at the Funambules on the Boulevard du Temple. He remained at this theatre, until his death. During this time he converted the crude slapstick form of Mime, to the art form that it is known as today. Deburau was a master of his art and was responsible for creating the lovesick 'Pierrot', the eternal seeker.

In 1921 at L'École du Vieux-Colombier, in Paris, France, Jacques Copeau, Charles Dullin, Etienne Decroux, Jean-Louis Barrault and others, explored and developed what became the new vision of mime. In this time period, movies brought us some of the greatest physical actors, Charles Chaplin and Buster Keaton.

During the following decades, this new, more refined mimetic discipline took different directions. Marcel Marceau, a student of Etienne Decroux was to become the most famous mime of all time.

Closer to our time, people like Claude St-Denis, Vincent Marcotte, Tony Montanaro, Bill Irwin, Rob Mermin, Robert Shield, and many others, are keeping the art of mime alive.

Now let's start studying your body.

Face

Exercises for face muscles and better expressions.

Eyebrows: Put your index over the eyebrow, then lift your eyebrow high enough to feel the movement with your finger. Do not use your finger to push. Only your eyebrow muscles are working.

Eyelids: Look straight in front of you then open your eyes wide by lifting the lids as much as you can, not using any other part of the face and relax. Repeat at least ten times. You might look scary.

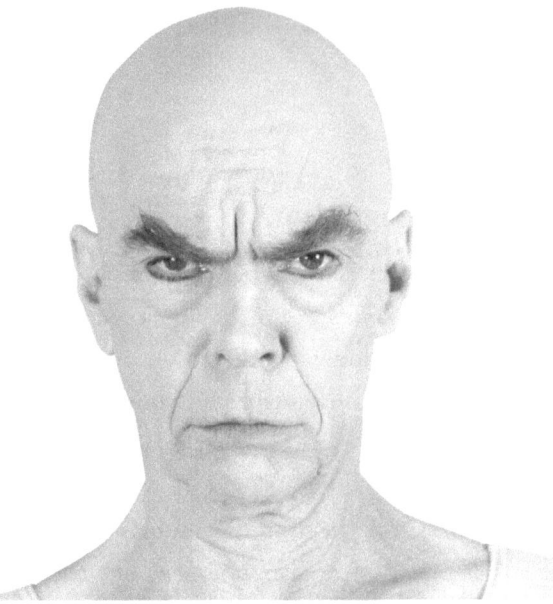

Fig. 1 - Eyebrows

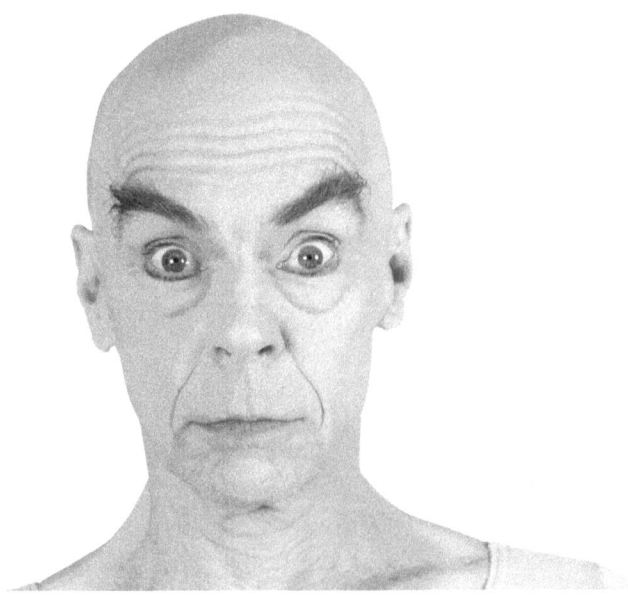

Fig. 2 - Eyebrows

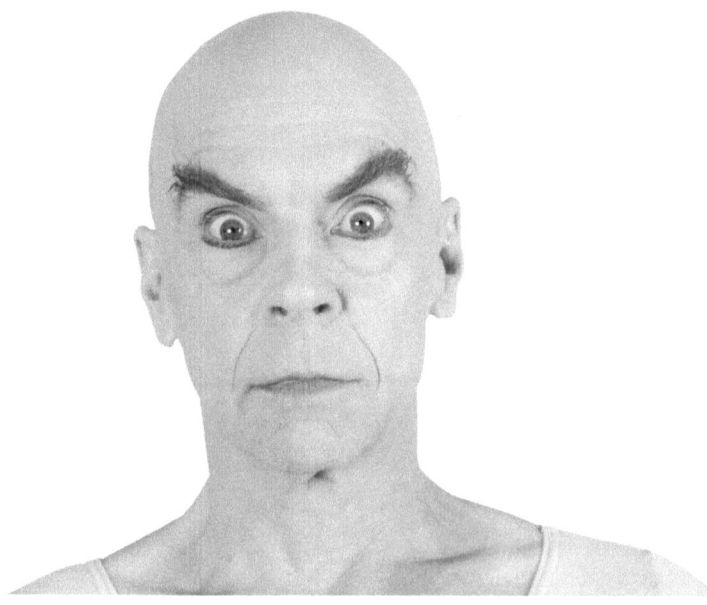

Fig. 3 - Eyelids

Lips and Face: Pronounce the vowels slowly using only the lips. Repeat the exercise using the jaws and then using the entire face. Make it big, and do not be afraid of exaggerating.

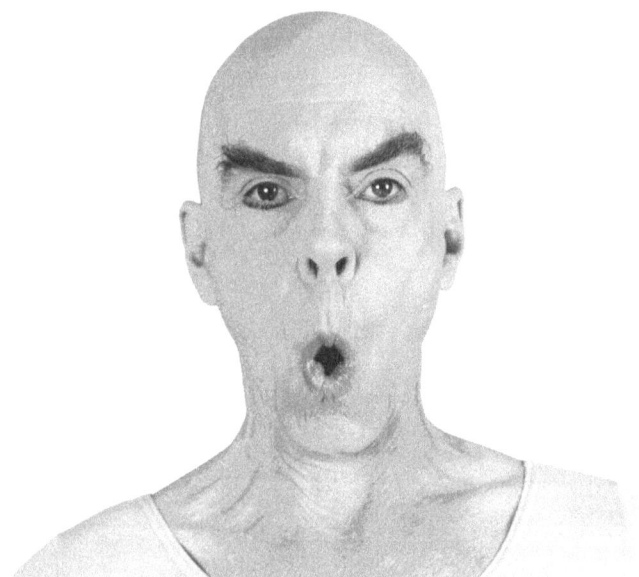

Fig. 4 - Vowel sounds

Fig. 5 - Vowel sounds

Fig. 6 - Vowel sounds

Now stand or sit in front of a mirror and study your face doing all the crooked and tortured expressions you can imagine. I suggest avoiding doing it in public.

When you understand how your face works, have fun reproducing every emotion you can think of.

Improvisation exercise:

You are sitting on a chair, relaxed. Your partner comes close to your ear and tells you secrets, which can be anything. Let your face react without control to whatever you hear.

Fig. 7 - Crooked and tortured

Fig. 8 - Crooked and tortured

HANDS

Exercises

To begin, a little warm-up of your fingers and hands is suggested.

The spider

On a wall or a table, reproduce the movements of a spider, using fingers as the legs. Do it very slowly to study how it works and then go convince someone it is actually a real, creepy bug. With time you can study different type of walks from different spiders.

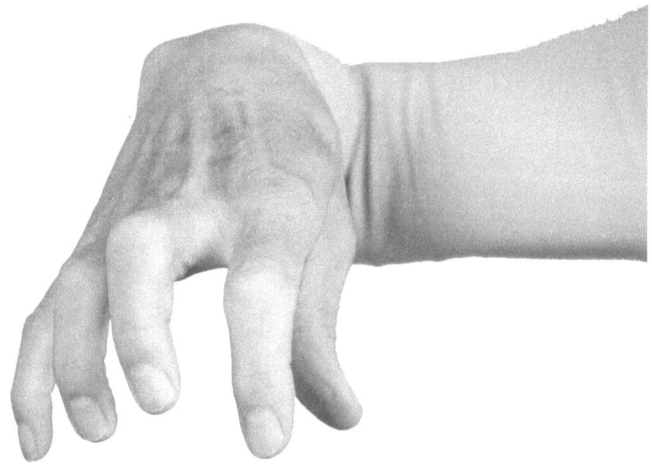

Fig. 9 - The spider

Waves

On a wall or a table, move your hands and fingers from the wrist to the tip of fingers until they look like small waves on the ocean. Then do it bigger, using elbows and shoulders. It will look like wings.

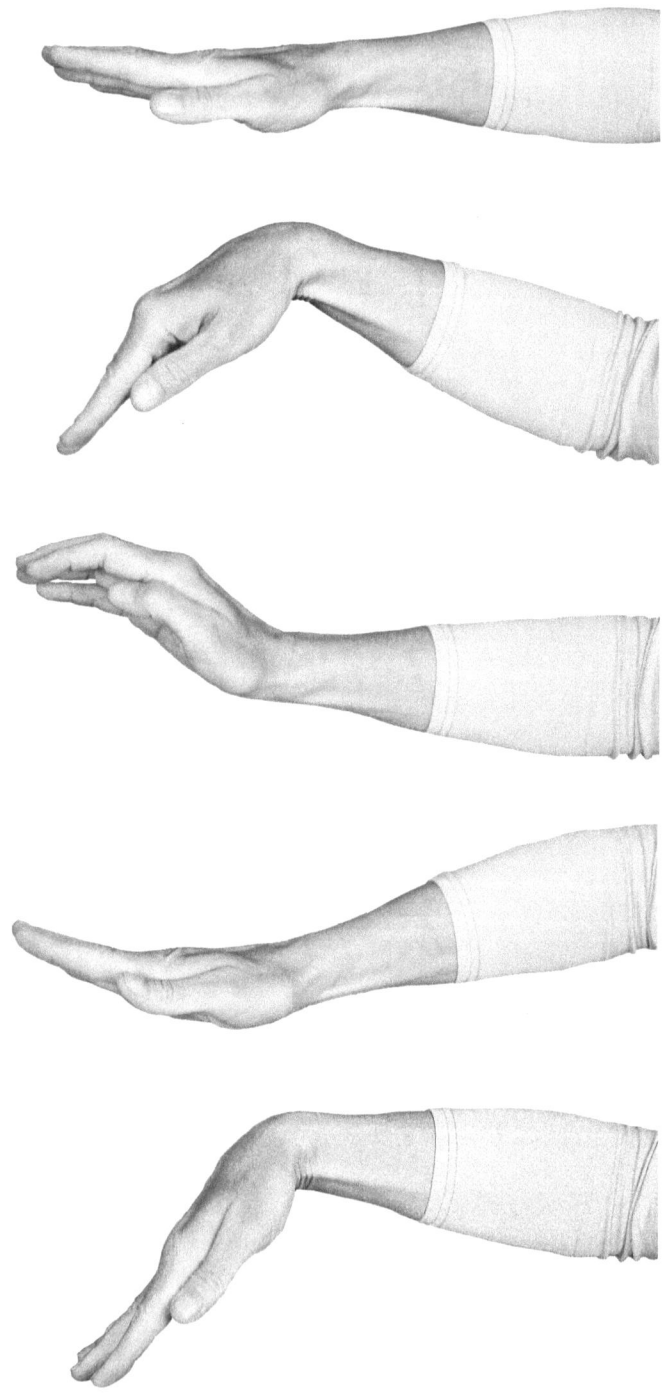

Fig. 10 - Waves

Fig. 11 - Hands in typical postures

Think of different situations, use your hands in typical postures. For example: pointing a finger to show authority, like your mother would do. Then be creative; begging hands, punching hands, waving goodbye, blowing kisses…

Study

Public areas are good for mime studies. Just sit somewhere, in a park or a shopping mall, and observe people around you. Look at their hands, how they move, and follow the words they say, or the emotions they show or hide. Hands can tell many things about who you are. On stage they become a very important part of you.

Body lines or Axes

Before anything else, let me explain the position zero.

Stand-up straight, feet together. Jump as you relax your legs. Your instinct should bring you back on the floor with heels 3 to 4 inches apart and the front of your feet half way opened. Keeping your feet fixed on the floor, move the rest of your body around, from side to side, back, front, until you feel in perfect balance. You are in position zero.

Definitions

In mime we divide the body in seven places and call them the seven axes. Each one can be used to express or demonstrate something like feelings, emotions, moods, your age, etc.

Axis number 1: The base of the head, or the chin

Fig. 12 - Axis 1

You will find it by doing mini-movements of the head in all directions. Like saying yes or no with hesitation. It is this axis I use to say things like "I am not sure" or "Hey what do you want, dude?" When a kid or a puppy wants something, and decides to look adorable, they break the head on the side with just a little movement. With this small movement, you fall for them.

Exercise

Find a partner and stand in front of each other. As you start moving around slowly, lift your chin to show superiority. Then your partner will do the same and a rooster fight will begin. The goal for both of you is to be taller and stronger than the other.

Axis number 2: The neck

Fig. 13 - Axis 2

You will find it by doing bigger "yesses" and bigger "nos", sliding head front and back like a pigeon, or side to side like in dances from India. With good training you can do 360 degrees sliding. It is used to show discouragement or shame or being very cute and also to exaggerate the movements of axis number 1.

Axis number 3: The solar plexus

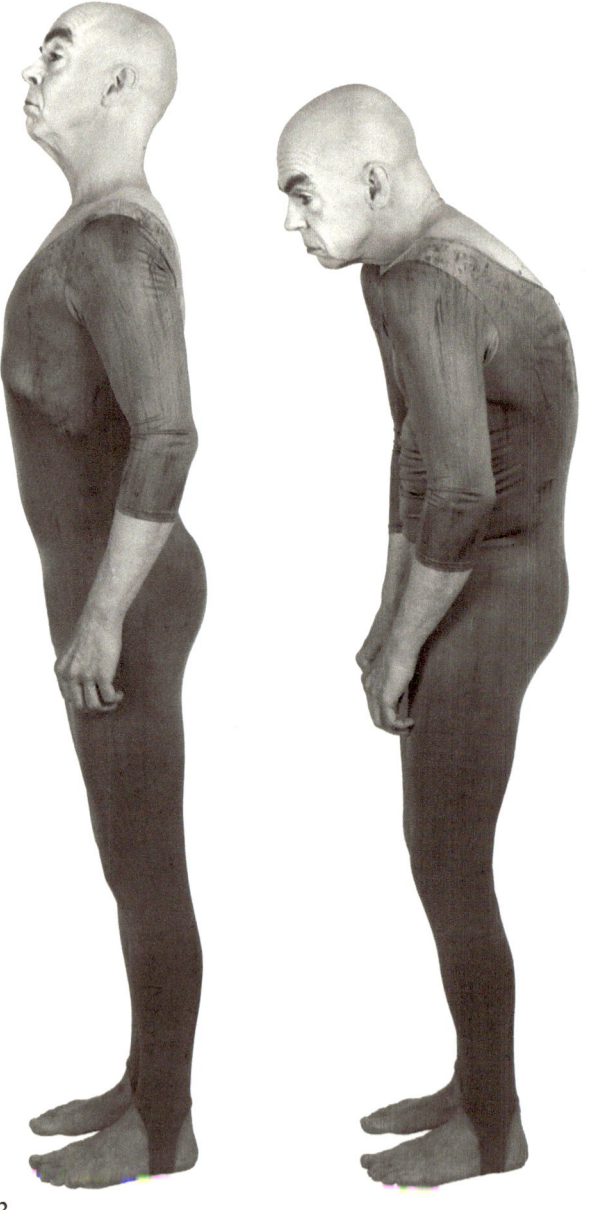

Fig. 14 - Axis 3

A little curve of your chest in front, from the back or from the side.

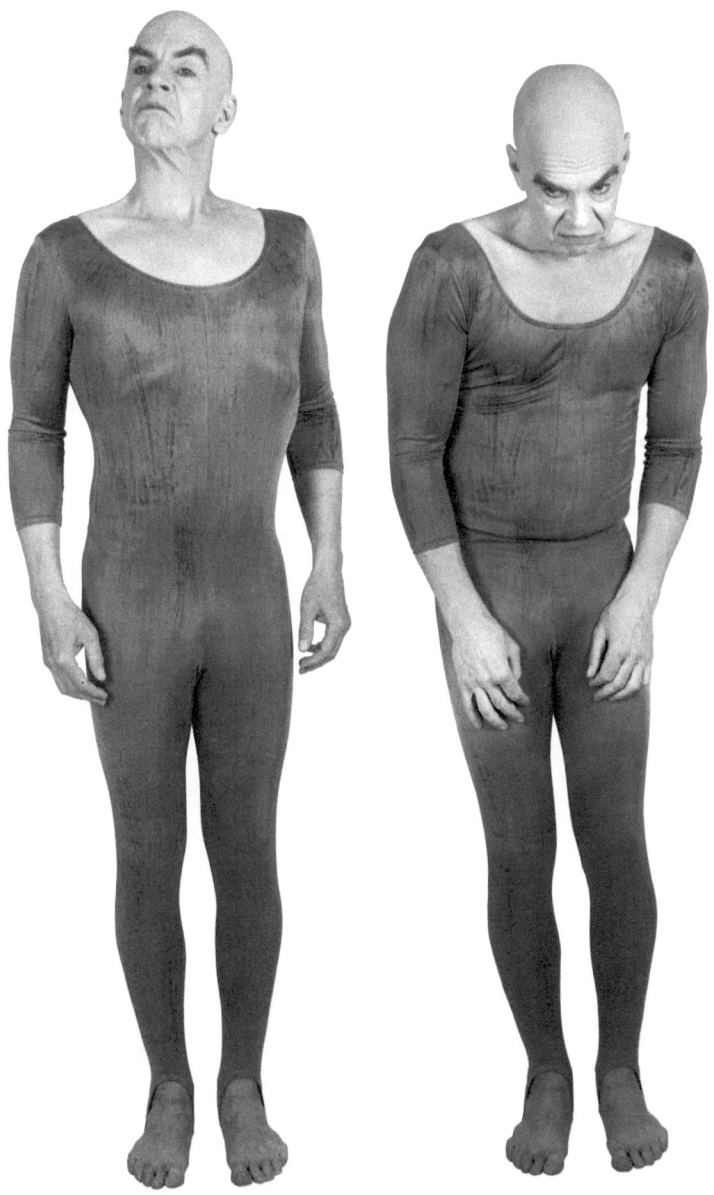

Fig. 15 - Axis 3 (front view)

Take a deep breath and lift your ribcage until it feels too much, that should give you a posture of power or pride. Breath out until you feel empty, this one should make you feel tired or older. Where my heart beats, where my chest grows as a teenage girl or boy. When I am proud or full of myself. When I am very shy or feel inferior or anxious. When I am beaten and destroyed or victorious and powerful. Chaplin was a master of this one. Look to the right, lift your right shoulder just a bit curving your rib cage to the right and here you are, you look cute and shy.

Axis number 4: The belly button and the waist

Imagine yourself getting punched directly in the belly. You would exhale and bend at the same time. In dance, the exercise is called contraction. You do this and then come back to a straight line and reverse your lower back to the front as if you become pregnant.

Using this body line, you can show fat belly, and different types of pain. Love hurt and Hara-kiri. Axis number 4 can be used to make axis number 3 look bigger, like being very tired or very old. It is useful when you play far from the audience.

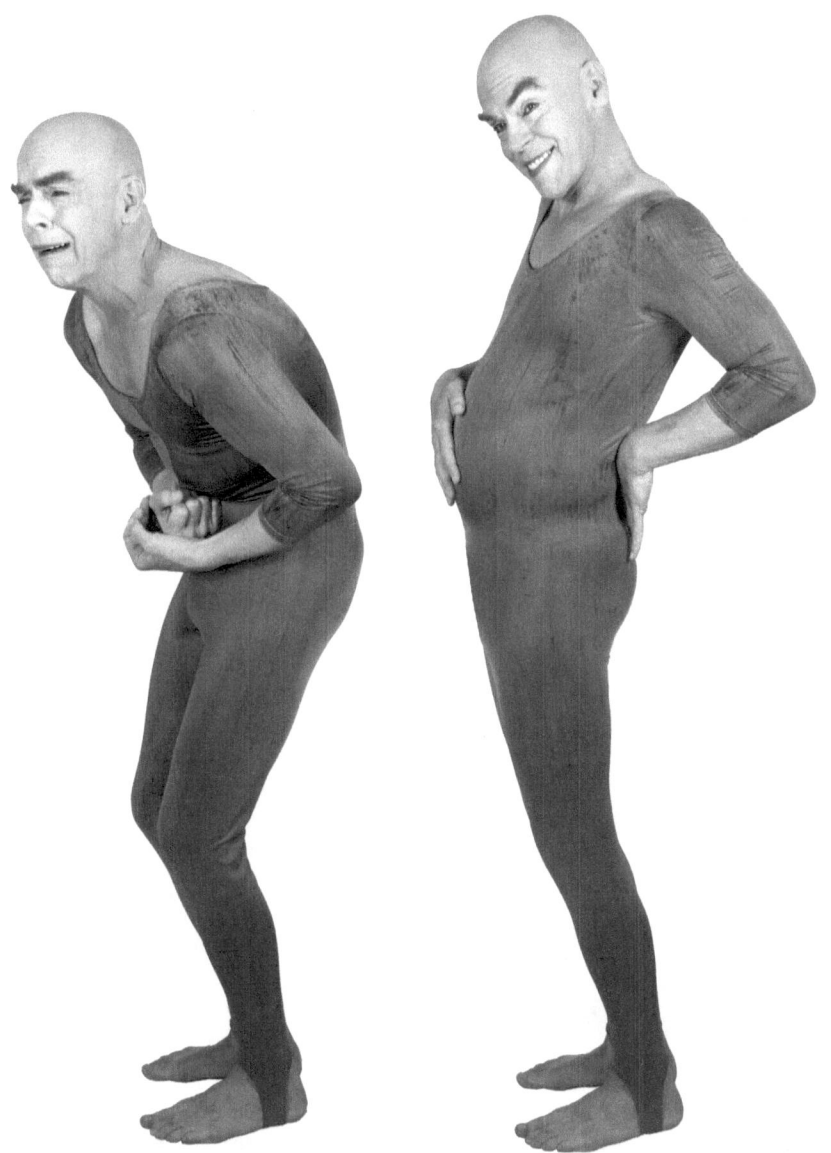

Fig. 16 - Axis 4

Axis number 5: The hips level

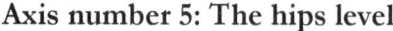

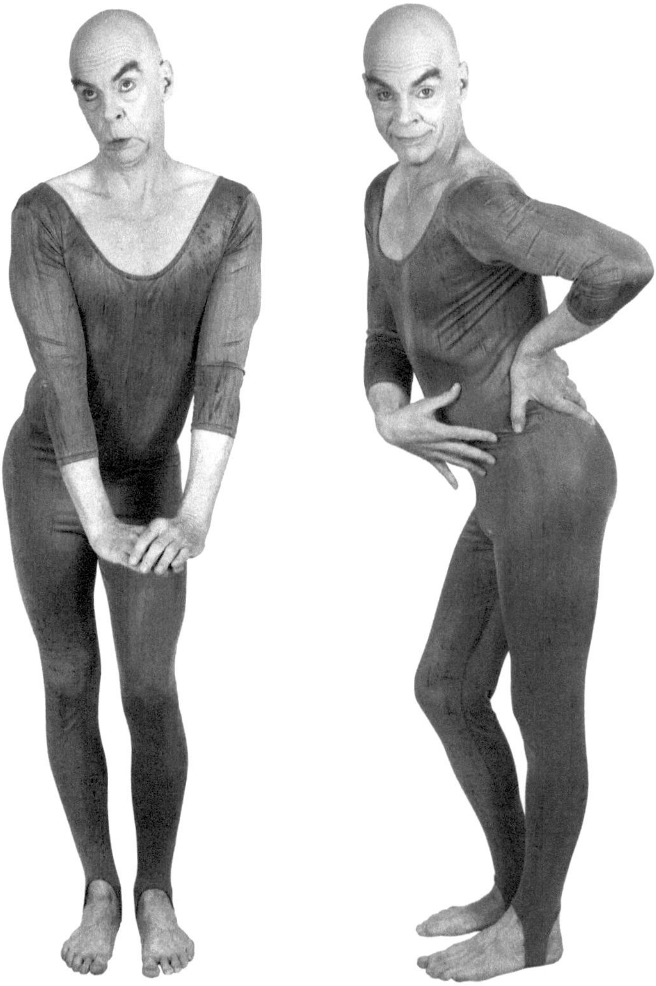

Fig. 17 - Axis 5

This is easy to find, as we all come from this area of the body. Move your hips around - back and forth, side to side. This is the axis of provocation, sensuality, sexuality and so many types of dance. It is used to show perversion as well as funny or twisted movements.

Axis number 6: The knees

Fig. 18 - Axis 6

Stand up in position zero, go up and down using only your knees, do little circles. We use the 6th axis to shrink or look heavier, walk like Godzilla or like a very old person. You can use it to look paralyzed, injured, or falling at someone's feet and imploring. You can go from a threatening gorilla to a weak person just by changing the angle of one knee.

Axis number 7: The feet and ankles

Same as the knees - use your feet to go up and down. Stand on one foot. With the other, practice to point and flex. Same exercise with both sides.

This last axis makes you look taller - light as a butterfly - graceful like a ballerina. Combine 6 and 7 to go from being heavy to light and from being stiff to a totally graceful person.

Exercises

From position zero, roll down slowly from the head and shoulders, following with torso, belly and hips. Bend your knees and ankles and touch your toes, then come back up slowly in position zero. Then think about situations where your body would be in these different alignments. With a partner, stand still like a dummy while the other person manipulates you. The partner will use each of the seven axes to transform your shape into a famous statue or sculpture, an animal or just to show your age or physical state.

Three things to remember:

Always warm up before practicing.
Always warm up before a show.
Always warm up.

Postures

Definition

The posture is the result of using the different axes to recreate a person, a thing, an animal, an illness, an emotion, or a state of mind. Posture can be used to create anything you want.

Exercises

Getting older: We all know someone old who can still run or dance. The goal of this exercise, however, is in the direction of stereotypes. Start at your age or younger and walk slowly, thinking of an aging body. Step by step, decade after decade. Getting tired and older, sick and much older, using your seven axes to recreate the different stages of life.

Waking up: opposite of getting older. Start asleep and take time to stand up and wake up. Then, move faster, taller, happier.

The growing tree: From Red Skelton, actor-clown-mime. This one is a total get-in-shape exercise.

You start little, from the seed, and grow slowly to a small tree with small branches, using your fingers as branches. Step by step you rise, fed by the sun. Your legs becoming the trunk, your arms being bigger branches, your fingers transform to leaves as the wind starts blowing. The use of all seven axes together can send emotions coming from the tree. From there, it gets cold and the tree gets older. The leaves are falling. Branches shrink and become crooked. Using both legs the opposite way, the tree is growing old and going back to the land. If you feel like it, you can use your face to incorporate emotions and make it an act.

Study

Again, public areas are a great school. Just sit and open your eyes. Watch people around you. How they walk, how they sit. The position of their feet, hands, heads. The way some will look around when others keep staring at the ground. Observe what happens when two persons or more get together. What body-lines they adopt in public.

(Did I mention to always warm up before anything physical?)

Energy and movement

The people before us - including Deburau, Decroux and Marceau - explored and observed the movement of every living creature. The result of their study was the four dynamics of movement. When you understand and control them, it becomes easy to reproduce whatever you want in motion and postures.

Dynamic number 1: Fondu

Fondu (or melting if you prefer) is a continuous movement that does not stop or start suddenly. It can be slow or fast, big or small. Someone running, walking in a dream, Tai-Chi movements can all be reproduced using the Fondu.

Exercises

Start walking slowly with normal movements. Then much slower making longer and bigger movements with your arms and legs. Come back to normal speed and then faster motion. Bring it back to super slow motion like you are in a dream or on the moon. All in continuous motion, no sudden stop or start.

Dynamic number 2: Toc

Toc is when the movement clearly stops or starts. Someone touches your shoulder and you jump. Someone calls your name and you freeze.

You are meditating and the phone rings. It looks like you are taking pictures.

Exercises

This one is easier to practice if you combine it with the Fondu. Walk slowly, making long motions with your legs and arms. Think about being in a photo session and every time you hear a click, you freeze. Then move again and freeze and keep doing it for a few minutes. Working with a partner, the other person will do the click sound and you will react to it. After a while, it will become easy to combine the Toc and Fondu to reproduce robotic movements.

Dynamic number 3: Rebound

Try to touch snail antennas, they will disappear before you can touch them and then they will come back in the same movement. No stopping. When you drop a ball, the moment it reaches the floor, it is already coming back up. Grab something burning and your hand will bounce automatically. You are going to fight or flirt with someone and at the last second, you change your mind and change direction. This is all the "rebound" dynamic.

Exercises

Walk like a basketball player. Walk normally and every few seconds, bounce like the ball in a game of pinball. Walk like a drunken person. With a partner, become slow motion boxers, using rebound dynamic when you hit and when you get hit. Other choice; a tennis game.

Dynamic number 4: Vibration

Small and fast movements with any segment of your body can be used to reproduce vibrations caused by fear, illness, cold, excitement, earthquake and more.

Exercises

Stand still in position zero. Concentrate on your legs and start shaking them for a few seconds. Then, add your butt muscles, your abdomen and torso, arms, shoulders, head… and stop. One minute of this is already a warm up.

Study

Now is time to go in public areas and pet shops. Analyze people you see around you. Are they very calm or just slow, nervous or energetic, paranoid, tired? Then, the animals, what is typical in the way they move? Which dynamics could you use to recreate their movements?

Oh! By the way, do not forget to warm up.

General Exercises

Chaplin

Just watching a Chaplin movie is already a great lesson. Using postures and dynamics, study how to transform your own body into Chaplin's character. You will see the use of axes - specifically 1-2-3 and 6. You will need the four dynamics including lots of bouncing. Do not forget all the face muscles.

Animals

After visiting a pet shop, find a private space to practice being an animal. It could be disturbing in a shopping mall. Just like anything else you plan to recreate, you will start by deciding in which dynamics they move, what are the typical bodylines you must use to find the right postures. Have fun with the faces. Some of them are really special.

Fig. 19 - Animals

Fig. 19 - Animals (cont.)

VISUAL EFFECTS

Fixed point

Definitions

A fixed point can be anywhere you imagine in the space. It becomes something when one hand or two are giving it a shape. The rest of your body is moving when the point is not. It is used for classics like the rope, the wall, the suitcase, the power lifter etc.

Mechanically speaking, your body is moving in a direction when the hand is moving the same distance in the opposite direction. This is where you are using counterweight. More specifically, you are holding something in your hand in a fixed point and then if your body goes 6 inches to the left, the fixed hand goes 6 inches to the right at the same time.

Exercises

Start with the real stuff. Go to a wall and feel it with your hands. Fix your hands on it as if they were stocked and move the rest of your body around them. Do the same with a real rope attached to something. Working fixed point with a partner can be fun as well. Shake hands and then, get stuck to each other.

Facing the mirror; the rope

In front of the mirror, reproduce the feeling you had on the wall and the rope. Watch your hands being fixed in the space. Move around or pull the rope, grab further and pull and grab and pull. Make it look heavier and harder to pull. Fondu and Toc will help amplify the illusion. Use different postures and facial expressions until you convince yourself. If you believe it, the audience will.

Fig. 20 - The rope

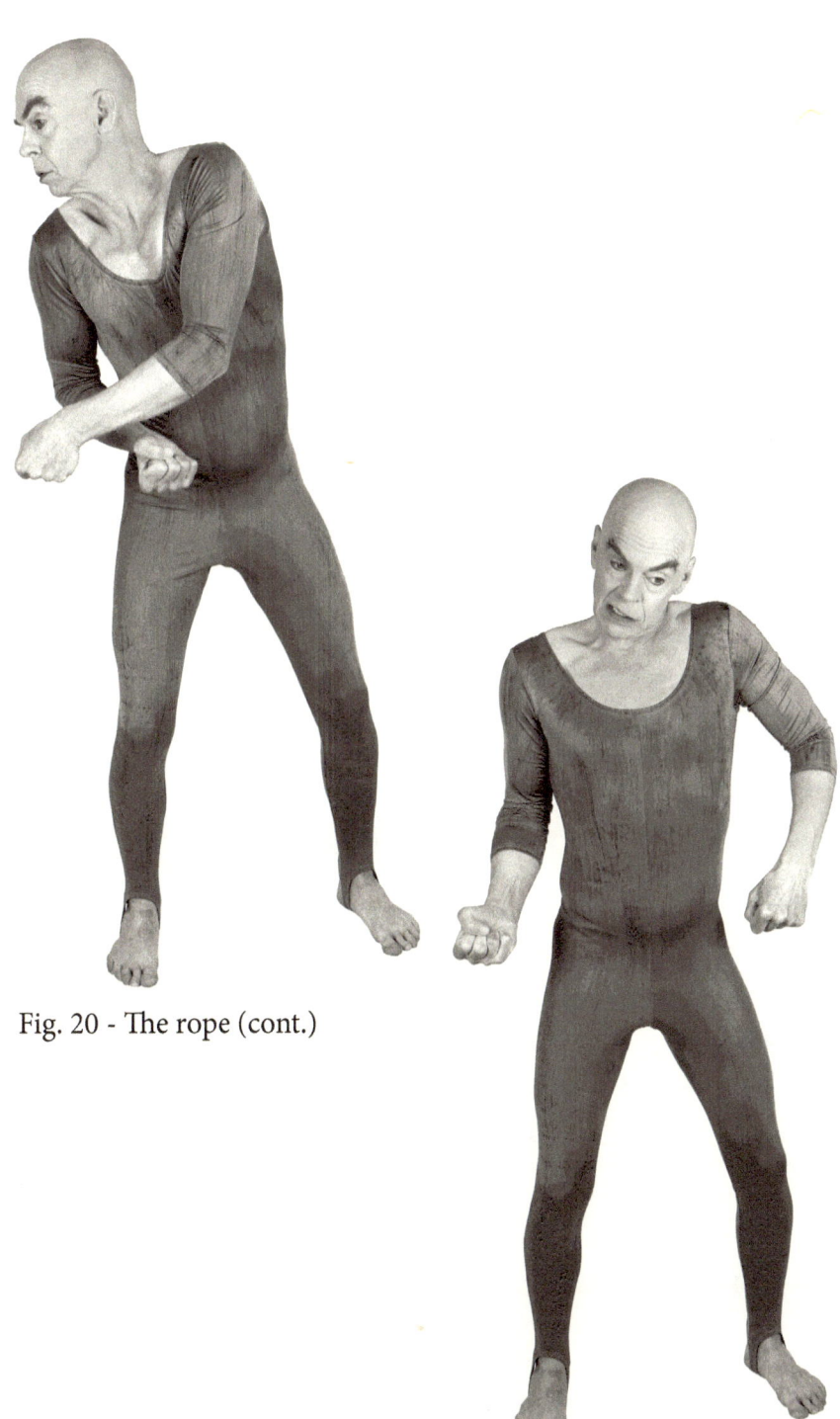

Fig. 20 - The rope (cont.)

Study

In the middle of the place, imagine a rope attached to the ceiling. Just like you did with the rope pulling, you will do rope climbing. Start seated on the floor. Grab the rope and pull yourself up inch by inch until you stand, and then keep going up stretching your body and using your feet (axis 7) to get higher. Always keep in mind that you are working on the fixed-point effect. You must keep the crowd focused on the rope.

The wall and the box

Same as mimes will use for the box or the elevator. Forget the mirror and start in the middle of nowhere. One hand after the other, create the first wall and then, three more walls. Make it a box including the top. When you feel comfortable with the technique, let the box shrink on you, wall after wall, until you are captive in a mini box. If you choose the elevator, instead of the shrinking effect, try to open it, pulling and pushing, pressing on the buttons and panicking.

Tug of war (group)

When you are with a group, transform the rope pulling exercise into a game of tug of war. Half the group sits and watches the other half competing. One of you becomes the silent referee. With the use of body language, the referee helps calling which side is stronger, then weaker and stronger again.

The walk

There are different mime walks developed and used by stage and street performers such as mimes, clowns and Hip-Hop dancers. The most famous is Michael Jackson but let's not forget Red Skelton, Marcel Marceau, James Brown and other great movers.

Exercises

My favorite way to learn and practice is the walk over tomatoes in the garden. Kids love it and it is easy to understand. Stand in front of your imaginary garden. Lift one foot and step over a tomato. Touch the ground with toes first and squish the tomato. Repeat with the second foot. Then do it again and again. Now it is time to add a technical detail. While the first foot squishes the tomato, the second one slides back in a brushing motion. It becomes squish and slide, squish and slide. You are still moving forward as you walk. Imagine the tomatoes being closer and closer to each other. Repeat the exercise until you walk in place.

With time and a better control of techniques, you will be able to create different illusions such as walking slow motion, in a dream, forward, backward, in place and of course, the moon walk.

Pantomime

Definition

Any dramatic or dancing performances in which a story is told, using expressive bodily or facial movements of the performers. To avoid subtitles as much as possible, most Charlie Chaplin movies were played in pantomime.

The suitcase

Using a real object can make things easier and help develop your techniques until you get to do anything you want without props. In the suitcase act you are using a real suitcase because the prop becomes a character. The story is yours. It could be a fight because you are trying to steal it or because that stubborn thing does not want to follow you. The facial expressions will make the difference. It could be a complicated love story between you and the suitcase. Technically speaking it is the same. You are using fixed point, counterweight, Fondu, Toc, Rebound and all axes available. The choice of dynamics is yours.

The mime enters the stage, sees the suitcase and goes to it. Trying to lift it, the mime realizes that it is very heavy. With a bit of work, the suitcase ends up in the air. The mime can go on. After a few steps, it stops in place and then, brings the mime back to point A. The mime is questioning his strength and tries again. The number of attempts is your choice. Make sure there is a build-up of efforts with the body and the facial expressions and different ways to lift it, push it and pull it. After succeeding in making more steps in the direction you wanted to go, decide if you win and bring it off stage or lose the fight and get pulled by the suitcase until you exit the wrong way.

Ringing the Bells

Is your fixed-point technique good? Your warm up is done? Do you have good balance? If so, you are ready to ring the bells. Your character could be a very old person or a meditating monk.

Your character enters the space. Once you have reached the rope, grab it firmly with both hands and start pulling down until the weight of the bell brings you back up. Do not forget to play sideways or with an angle so the audience can see clearly your hands and face. The efforts you make against the weight of the bell should show in your face as much as in your bodylines. The use of the rebound and vibration dynamics will complete the effect of the bell movements and sounds.

In the classic version, the bell takes you of the ground, which means good control of the seventh axes. It means too, that ringing the bell makes you younger, lighter and happier. When you are done, your body comes back to what it was and leaves… in peace.

Fig. 20 - Ringing the bells

Fig. 20 - Ringing the bells (cont.)

The Flower (The Daisy)

Here comes the perfect pantomime exercise to use all your face muscles, your hands, fingers and bodylines, more specifically the upper body (axes 1-2-3).

You all know the story. One petal says "They love me!" One says "They love me not!" It is a simple game between you and the daisy.

Enter the stage and search for the perfect flower. Pick it and bring it close to your face to admire it. When you begin questioning your love situation, start with small expressions, short movements and small Toc on the petals. You feel good when love is there. It is not so bad when love is not there. Petal after petal, make the reactions bigger with the face and the hands. Never forget, you are playing for an audience. Your hands should never be right in front of your face. Even if the movements are small, keep them distant or on the sides.

After a couple more petals, your expressions, your movements and your bodylines are becoming bigger and bigger. To the point where we think you can fly with love or you are going to die if the last petal says "They love me not!"

You decide if the story will be funny or dramatic, sad or intense. This is your life after all.

Fig. 21 - The flower

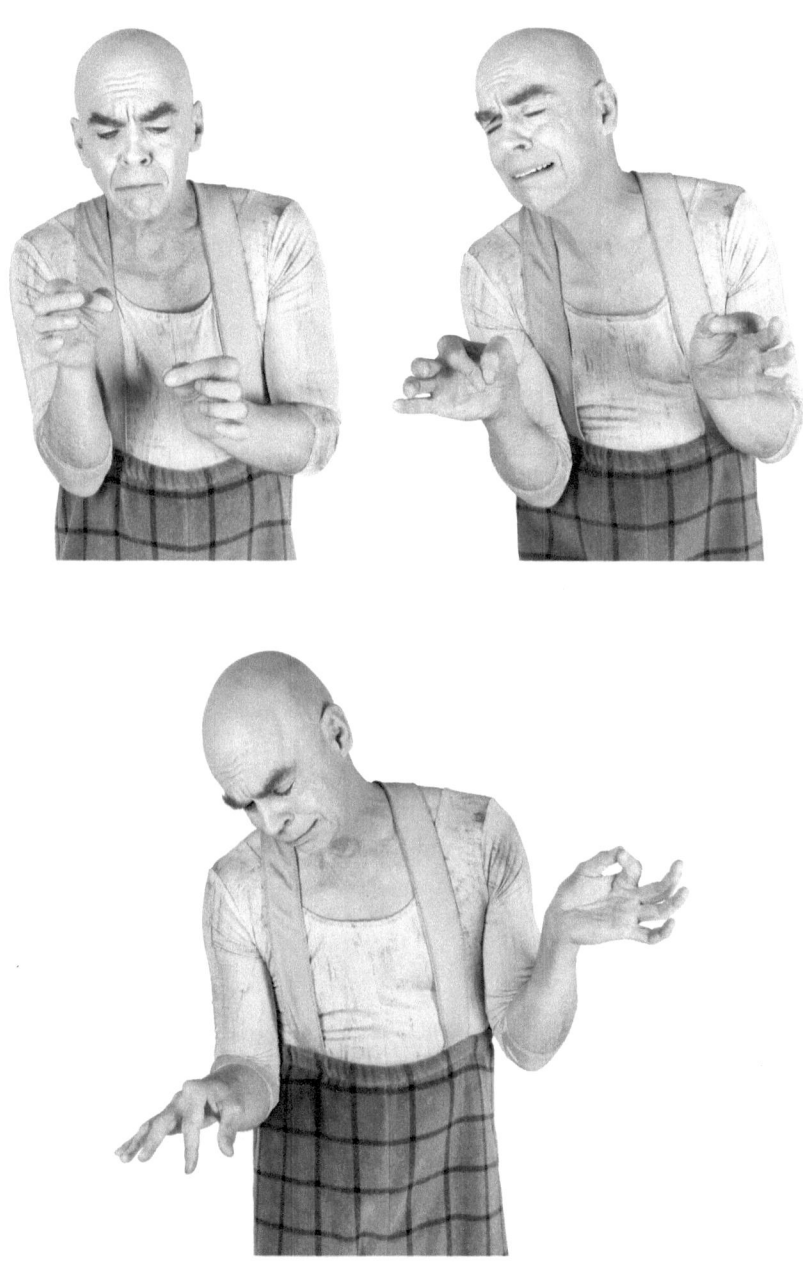

Fig. 21 - The flower (cont.)

The Tight Wire

Watching Charlie Chaplin's *The Circus* could be inspiring before playing the tight wire. This is the opposite of the daisy - this one will makes you work with your legs more than anything else. You need mostly the rebound dynamic for each segment of the body.

The story is simple, you walk from A to B hoping not to fall and die. When that is done, you come back the same way from B to A. The rest is at your convenience.

Are your nervous, glorious or totally drunk on the wire? Maybe you are trying to flirt with someone in the crowd when it can be deadly to look down. A bird could disturb your performance. Many tight rope walkers will use an umbrella, a stick or a feather to help their balance. Then, of course, you will dance and jump and turn to impress the audience.

All this keeping in mind that for each step or action there will be a few bouncing motions in your knees, arms and head. After being successful, you can exit the stage with pieces of your body still bouncing.

Fig. 22 - Tight wire

The Power Lifter

Bring all your face and body muscles and all the testosterone you can imagine. You are at the Olympic games, competing in power lifting. Before entering the space, choose if you want to be as large as a sumo or in the smaller and lighter Welterweight category. Then bring with you, facial expressions, the seven axes, the four dynamics, and the fixed point technique.

The athlete enters the space, focused, intense and looking at the weights. Breathing like a yogi, the muscle machine grabs the barbell one hand after the other and looks straight in front.

First attempt, it seems too heavy. The body is moving but the weights are not. Attempt missed. The athlete comes back in a straight position, breathing deeply. Putting more chalk on both hands, we can see the determination.

The giant is back. Showing the same focused face and putting a stronger grip on the barbell. We can see how much power will get out of these muscles.

Second attempt, the bar gets off the floor easily. We can see the legs bouncing and the eyes searching as the champion gets stuck with the weights at the chest level. The bar falls back on the floor. The rebound dynamic with your head will make the audience see the weights bouncing on the floor. Attempt missed.

Back to the chalk box to cover hands and arms, the monster turns to the weights with rage, breathes like a buffalo and walks like a wrestler.

Third and last attempt, our big winner grabs and lifts the weights in the same motion and pushes and pushes until the bar gets stuck again in the air over the head level. The athlete analyzes the situation, then leaves the weights in the air, goes to the chalk box, covers the hands, arms and shoulders with chalk, comes back and pushes the bar to the top. Third attempt succeeded.

You could end it there, drop the barbell and bow, or give it a funnier finally having to fight to bring the weights back on the floor.

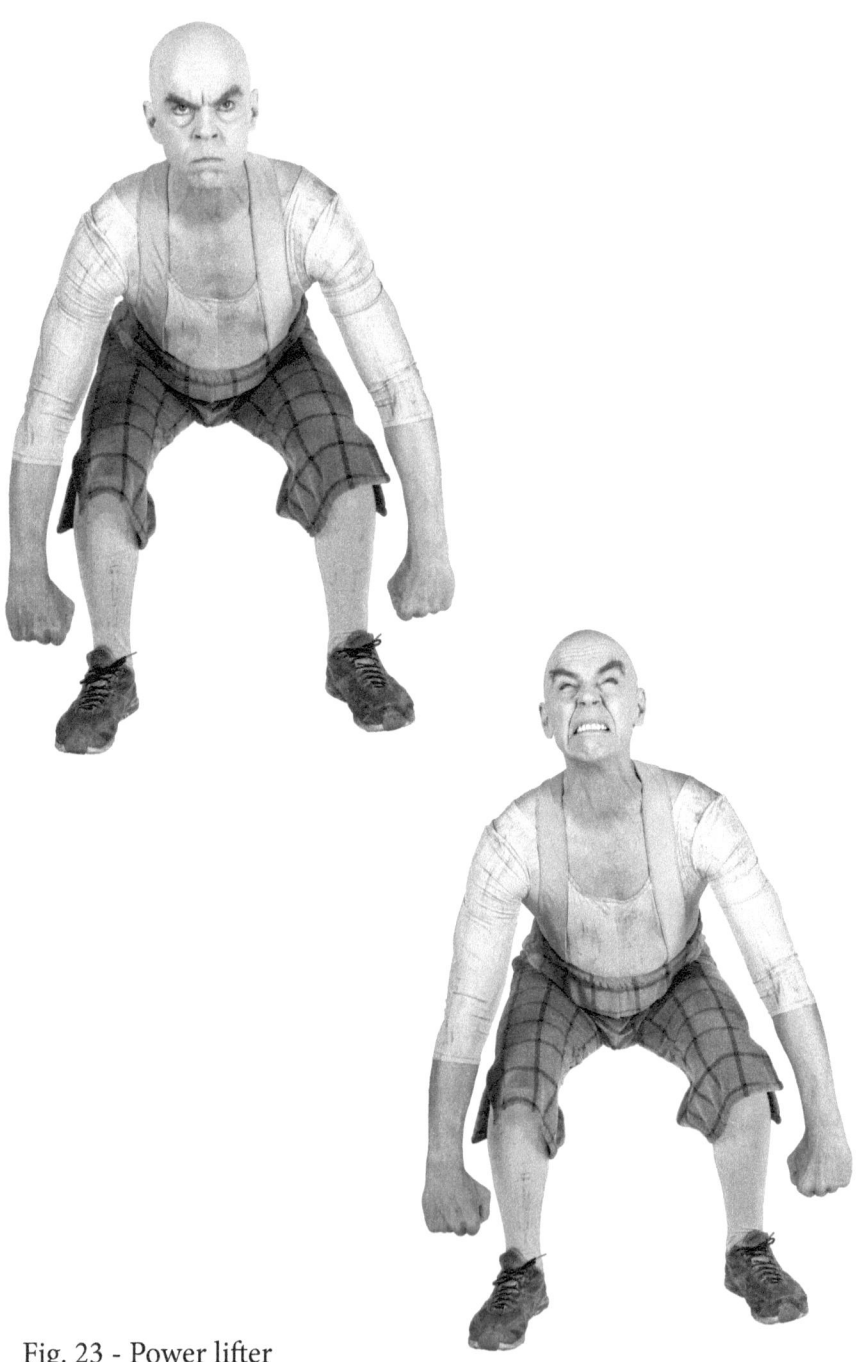

Fig. 23 - Power lifter

Fig. 23 - Power lifter (cont.)

The Chair (duet)

There is a real chair on stage, but only one. There are two mimes coming on stage from both sides. They need to sit, both of them. Problems!

The act is easy to understand, there will be a competition to earn the right to sit on the only chair available.

Both mimes are fundamentally polite. One after the other, the characters will refuse to sit and offer the place politely and more politely and more and more. The goal here is to build up with extreme kindness, exaggerated smiles and immense movements of the whole body until one of the mimes loses patience.

From there, the game reverses to an aggressive fight, with both mimes trying to convince one another to take the chair and sit. The same build-up of gestures and facial expressions as before, with the difference that everything becomes rude.

In the version I used to play with my mentor, a third person would come, reading a newspaper, oblivious to the other two. This third person would sit on our chair and read quietly. And us? We left the stage holding each other and crying.

This piece is a pantomime and can be played with a mime and a ballerina. The build-up becomes a demonstration of the dance language compared to the mime language. It can be done with many other physical artistic disciplines.

Improvisation

The Mirror (duet)

With your partner and facing each other, you are the mover and the other is the reflection. Move slowly to allow your partner to follow easily. Make small and long movements. Change direction. Change your bodylines and facial expressions. After a few minutes, switch roles.

Character Walks (solo)

Start walking normally. After a few seconds, change to an old man, then a young woman, a drunkard, a kid playing, Godzilla walking all over a city, and then... keep transforming as long as your imagination will feed you.

One Thing Leading to Another (solo)

Imagine an object that transforms into something else - this will happen as many times as you want. Each object will connect with the next one in some way, and that will bring your character to adapt to the change with expressions and bodylines. For example, you are walking with a cane, the cane becomes an umbrella, the umbrella becomes a rifle, the rifle becomes a fishing pole that becomes a baseball bat, and then it becomes an axe and so on and so on.

Have fun, be creative.

Silence is talking to you.

About the Author

Born in 1958 in Louiseville, Canada, Mario Diamond discovered mime while studying literature in college. In 1976 Mario was on stage for the first time. Four decades later, this mime has performed over 10,000 shows in Europe, Asia, South and North America. He has also played in television shows, movies and TV commercials.

Always captivated by the silent art, Mario developed his own style and teaching techniques to apply in physical acting with circus performers, actors, figure skaters and politicians. It is a three step technique; learn, practice, apply.

For more information about Mario Diamond, visit his website
www.mimemario.com

Other Titles by Modern Vaudeville Press

Juggling - From Antiquity to the Middle Ages
by Thom Wall
ISBN: 978-0578410845

As with dance, so with juggling—the moment that the performer finishes the routine, their act ceases to exist beyond the memory of the audience. There is no permanent record of what transpired, so studying the ancient roots of juggling is fraught with difficulty. Using the records that do exist, juggling appears to have emerged around the world in cultures independent of one another in the ancient past.

Paintings in Egypt from 2000 BCE show jugglers engaged in performance. Stories from the island nation of Tonga place juggling's creation with their goddess of the underworld—a figure who has guarded a cave since time immemorial. Juggling games and rituals are pervasive in isolated Inuit cultures in northern Canada and Greenland.

Winner of Next Generation Indie Book Awards - "Best Nonfiction eBook" 2019

A friend once asked me, 'What's the point of juggling three or five balls?' None, really, besides that not everybody can do it. Yet, juggling is one of humanity's oldest performing arts; it seems that every civilization known to man has produced amazing people who have successfully tried to keep objects moving simultaneously in the air in defiance of all laws of gravity. So, where does juggling comes from? When did it begin? What is its history? These are the questions Thom Wall has endeavored to answer in his fascinating book, Juggling From Antiquity To The Middle Ages. Thoroughly researched, richly illustrated, Thom Wall's book is a must-read for anyone interested in juggling or the circus arts in general, anyone interested in performing arts, and anyone with a curious mind.

- Dominique Jando, author, The Circus (1870-1950)

Juggling or: How to Become a Juggler (annotated edition)
By Rupert Ingalese & Thom Wall
ISBN: 978-1-7339712-0-1

Juggling or How To Become a Juggler: the annotated edition is another piece of juggling literature from Modern Vaudeville Press aimed at increasing the fact-checked and scholarly approach to understanding the history of juggling. Thom Wall, author of *Juggling: From Antiquity to the Middle Ages* and professional juggler, annotates a re-release of one of the earliest books written to share information for approaching juggling as a profession by Rupert Ingalese.

Two special gifts are received from reading this book. First, we are presented with an opportunity to read a manual written by a professional juggler in 1921. These chapters contain stories of old variety performers, anecdotes of personal growth learned in the art of juggling, and revelations of how similar the professional world of the performing artist is to today's industry.

Second, our 'humble editor' Wall, gives footnotes addressing the inconsistencies presented as 'fact' as well as clarifies terminology or references that us early 21st century readers will not understand as immediately as an early 20th century reader. Wall uses primary source evidence instead of relying on personal anecdotes or assumptions helping our art form grow academically alongside the artistic and cultural work being done. The footnotes happen purposefully and are presented in a guiding and mentor-like voice, creating a sense of trust between editor and reader. I found myself excited to find another footnote and hear another bit of information as though I were piecing together a puzzle of juggling history.

Juggling or How To Become a Juggler: the annotated edition is a welcomed addition to any juggler's (or historian's) library by connecting jugglers of today to the jugglers of the past. Any teacher of juggling would benefit from reading the book to know some of the earliest standards of transmitting the skill and Wall's additions aid in accurately passing along our artform's technical history.

- Benjamin Domask - CircusTalk.com

If you enjoyed *Body Talk - Basic Mime*, you might be interested in *What Scientists Have to Say About Juggling*. A 15-page treatise on the current state of juggling research. This Amazon bestselling booklet outlines juggling and its effects on the practitioner's body and mind.

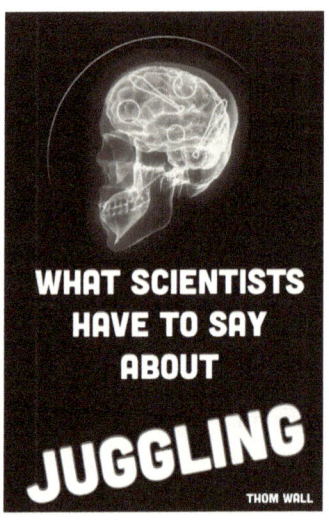

Now available as a free digital download!
http://thomwall.com/sciencebook

"The nerdiest non-nerdy explanation of the current state of juggling research in the world. Super legit content, mixed with light touch of humor."

Craig Quat: www.quatprops.com

"This ebook covers an incredible amount of research while keeping the information engaging and useful for a juggling practice. I have been either training, performing, or teaching juggling for about two decades, and I learned a ton! Whether you're just discovering an interest in juggling or you're far down the rabbit hole, read this today."

Jeremy Fein: www.feinmovement.com

"This paper is in-depth, interesting, and informative. Thom has dug up some of the juiciest academic and scientific tidbits of our art to help legitimize and de-stigmatize the word "juggler." Time spent reading this book will not only deeply intrigue the casual reader but help facilitate the education potentials of teachers and hobbyists alike."

Benjamin Domask: www.benjamindomask.com

www.ingramcontent.com/pod-product-compliance
Lightning Source LLC
Chambersburg PA
CBHW060505080526
44584CB00015B/1554